GIUSEPPE SANTAMARIA

New York Style

LOOK,
SHOP, EAT
& PLAY

AS
GUIDED BY
LOCALS

Smith
Street
Books

Introduction

*Like many, my infatuation with
New York City stemmed from notable
television shows, films and books, which have
told the city's story a thousand times over.
Before I'd even set foot in the New York, they
gave me a certain sense of what it would be like.*

In June 2006, I finally went there. I was twenty years old,
fresh out of college and had travelled over the border from my
native Canada to intern at *V*, a Downtown fashion magazine. A film
featuring a certain Hollywood actress debuted that same year,
and to say that my experience of working at a popular magazine
mimicked that film's protagonist's would be accurate.

I didn't end up staying long, as life had other plans for me;
specifically, living and loving in Sydney, Australia. But that
didn't keep me away from the city I'd fallen in love with first.

I've been fortunate in my career as a photographer to visit
New York every year since 2006, and subsequently capture an
outsider's perspective of the city's ever-evolving style through
the dress sense and attitude of real New Yorkers on the street.

As much as I noticed the city change with each visit, the soul
of it has stayed the same - and I strongly believe that's thanks
to the great mix of people who inhabit it.

My latest trip, sixteen years to the month of that
first visit, with camera and notebook in tow, was to capture
familiar places and talk to new faces about where they like to
look, shop, eat and play - New-York style.

GIUSEPPE SANTAMARIA

Contents

Along with recommendations by stylish locals on the streets of Downtown Manhattan, Williamsburg and north-west Brooklyn, you'll find neighbourhood walks that highlight old and new favourites. Or, if you're in a certain mood, pick a vibe.

WILLIAMSBURG BRIDGE
DELANCEY ST AND CLINTON ST, LOWER EAST SIDE

"There's an underhang for two on the Williamsburg Bridge that overlooks the Lower East Side. It's a bit scary, but it has sick views – Google it."

DONTA IN SOHO

LOWER EAST SIDE

REGINA'S GROCERY
27 ORCHARD ST, LOWER EAST SIDE

"I love eating at Regina's on the Lower East Side – the 'Uncle Jimmy' is bomb."

RAE IN THE LOWER EAST SIDE

LOWER EAST SIDE

PLAY

BAKER FALLS
101 AVENUE A, EAST VILLAGE

"Baker Falls in the East Village. It's a good place to let out some energy. It's where the Pyramid Club used to be."

JOHNNY IN THE WEST VILLAGE

Lower East Side

The Lower East Side was previously known for its locally owned Asian eateries and secondhand electronic goods. But an injection of new blood is giving a fresh take on this old-school downtown neighbourhood.

1. ENTRANCE 2. LAUNCH PHOTO BOOKS AT FOLEY GALLERY
3. METROGRAPH NYC 4. SARGENT'S DAUGHTERS 5. BODE
6. CAFÉ FORGOT 7. COLBO 8. TOP HAT 9. DIMES
10. MEL THE BAKERY 11. SCARR'S PIZZA 12. NORTH DUMPLING
13. UP STAIRS 14. SWAN ROOM 15. RECEPTION BAR
16. OLD MAN HUSTLE COMEDY BAR L.E.S

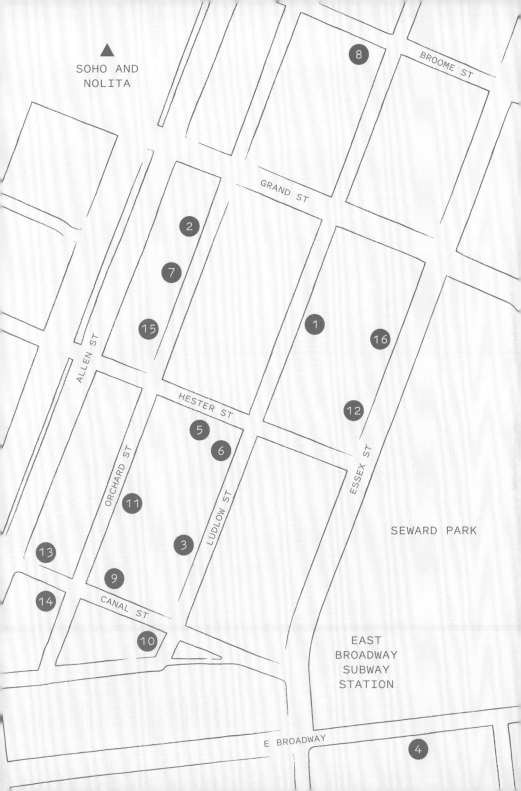

LOOK

ENTRANCE
48 LUDLOW ST
This artist-run space serves as a community clubhouse, with a gallery up front and a raw space out back used as a residency studio for artists during show runs.

LAUNCH PHOTO BOOKS AT FOLEY GALLERY
59 ORCHARD ST
Photography-related events are run regularly at the bookstore-inside-a-gallery, where you'll no doubt be inspired by the artists in the pages of the books, as well as the art on the walls and the talented artists themselves.

METROGRAPH NYC
7 LUDLOW ST
This old-Hollywood-style independent movie theatre focuses on rare archival screenings on 35mm and digital. Plus, it also has a charming restaurant, two bars, a bookstore and a candy shop.

SARGENT'S DAUGHTERS
179 EAST BROADWAY
An engaging and imaginative exhibition space with a strong female presence in its program, this gallery often highlights overlooked artists working outside of the established art world.

SHOP

BODE
58 HESTER ST
If you've got coin to spend on beautifully made, limited-edition beaded harlequin trousers or patchwork lace shirts, Emily Bode's wood-clad HQ is a great place to find unique investment pieces that are grounded in classic menswear.

CAFÉ FORGOT
29 LUDLOW ST
At this shopper's paradise, one-of-a-kind pieces from independent designers are displayed on an epic rotating rack reminiscent of Cher Horowitz's closet.

COLBO
51 ORCHARD ST
Speaking of variety, Colbo is just as much a clothing boutique as it is an art gallery, coffee shop and record store. Excellently curated, it's easy to spend a whole afternoon here.

TOP HAT
245 BROOME ST
World traveller Nina Allen's curation of whimsical knick-knacks are mostly from manufacturers who've been around for 100 years or more.

EAT

MEL THE BAKERY
1 LUDLOW ST
Specialising in sourdough
that's baked in their
basement, Mel's selection
of breads and pastries
is impressive. The olive
and pine nut focaccia, in
particular, is everything!

SCARR'S PIZZA
22 ORCHARD ST
They're known for the best
plain slice in New York,
but it's the pepperoni
and jalapeño Sicilian
drizzled with hot honey
that will blow your mind.
Grab a seat at the bar, or
a booth in the back for a
great late-night hang.

DIMES
49 CANAL ST
This eatery's opening in
2014 prompted a change
in the area as more non-
resident-owned restaurants
popped up. A separate
Dimes deli and market soon
followed, giving this
end of Canal Street the
nickname Dimes Square.

NORTH DUMPLING
27A ESSEX ST
The ginger pork and chive
dumplings have a dedicated
following, so expect a
line of hungry regulars.
Once you get yours, grab
a bench in Seward Park
across the street.

PLAY

UP STAIRS
59 CANAL ST
In keeping with the spirit
of the neighbourhood's past,
end the night (or start
the day?) at this cheap
and cheerful karaoke bar
located on the second floor
of a building with a bright
pink fire escape and a
hole-in-the-wall entrance.

SWAN ROOM
54 CANAL ST
At the opposite end of the
spectrum is a spot that's
new to the neighbourhood
but steeped in history.
Part of the redevelopment
of a century-old former
bank, it's now home to
Nine Orchard, a fancy
hotel, and its Swan Room.
Dress up for a night out.

RECEPTION BAR
45 ORCHARD ST
Cocktails and non-alcoholic
elixirs using traditional
Korean ingredients - think
fruity and botanical
flavours - take pride of
place on the menu here.

OLD MAN HUSTLE
COMEDY BAR L.E.S
39 ESSEX ST
Bars like this are what
make the Lower East Side
the Lower East Side. Cheap
booze and a variety of
comedy shows will keep you
entertained all night.

PLAY

"Attaboy in the Lower East Side is my favourite spot for a cocktail. It's a discreet place with a black door outside that you have to look out for. There is no menu; you just let the waiter know what kind of flavours you like and they'll custom-make you a drink."

CALVIN IN THE LOWER EAST SIDE

LOWER EAST SIDE

WING ON WO & CO.
26 MOTT ST, CHINATOWN

"I grew up in China, so I like to be in Chinatown. Going into the ritual stores makes me feel a bit more connected to my roots."

WENXUAN IN WILLIAMSBURG

LOWER EAST SIDE

SHOP

VINTAGE DISTRICT
LOWER EAST SIDE, BELOW EAST HOUSTON

*"I love shopping for vintage stuff
in the Lower East Side – it's like what
SoHo used to be."*

BRI IN THE EAST VILLAGE

If you're like me and nostalgic for the New York of times gone by, visit one of these vintage shops to find a piece of it.

VIBE

I miss the old New York

LEISURE CENTRE
48 HESTER ST
With a constant refresh of recherché and relevant clothing and objects from the late 20th century, you'll discover a treasure each time you visit.

10 FT SINGLE BY STELLA DALLAS
285 NORTH 6TH ST
Endless racks of well-loved and deadstock pieces are colour-coded and separated by function.

DESERT VINTAGE
34 ORCHARD ST
A fanciful boutique, carrying a well-curated selection of 70s YSL and 90s Comme des Garçons.

WHAT GOES AROUND COMES AROUND
351 WEST BROADWAY
Dubbed "the Bergdorf's of vintage stores", here you'll find coveted handbags from the last fifty years.

ENDING SOON
254 BROOME ST
Contemporary classic wear: think late-90s red carpet, Gianni Versace Istante pinstripe suits and Jil Sander pointed-toe boots.

ROGUE
53 STANTON ST
Founded by Gen-Z-er Emma Rodelius, this place is all about nostalgia-core and Y2K, making it all very accessible.

WEST VILLAGE

BETWEEN W 14TH ST AND W HOUSTON ST

"The Village: I love being around here. It feels small."

SERGIO IN THE WEST VILLAGE

SOHO AND NOLITA

CITY OPERA THRIFT SHOP
513 W 26TH ST, CHELSEA

*"I love thrifting all over the city.
My favourite is City Opera Thrift Shop.
You can get everything there."*

GREGORY IN THE WEST VILLAGE

NOLITA AND SOHO

COMPANY GALLERY
145 ELIZABETH ST, SOHO

"Company Gallery has some incredible emerging artists that build these worlds. It's something to see!"

ISI IN SOHO

SoHo & Nolita

These two neighbourhoods sitting south of Houston Street have become famous over the past decade for drawing tourists to their designer boutiques and chain stores. These days, a mix of old and new establishments are bringing a stylish crowd back to the streets.

1. ELIZABETH STREET GARDEN 2. NEW MUSEUM 3. TIWA SELECT
4. SOHO STREETS 5. 3SIXTEEN NY 6. AIMÉ LEON DORE
7. MCNALLY JACKSON BOOKS 8. NOLITA MARKET 9. LA ESQUINA
10. JACK'S WIFE FREDA 11. FANELLI CAFE 12. LITTLE PRINCE
13. BOTANICA 14. THE GARRET COCTELERÍA
15. CLUB ROOM AT THE SOHO GRAND HOTEL 16. JIMMY

LOOK

ELIZABETH STREET GARDEN
ELIZABETH ST

You can find solitude in this hidden oasis in the middle of Nolita. Located between Prince and Spring streets, the community garden is decorated with sculptures and is open year-round to the public.

NEW MUSEUM
235 BOWERY

You really never know what you're going to see when you enter this contemporary art gallery, but it's sure to be something wild!

TIWA SELECT
181 MOTT ST

Gallerist Alex Tieghi-Walker celebrates artists with non-conventional art backgrounds, showcasing their work in a space that's just as unconventional.

SOHO STREETS
BETWEEN WEST HOUSTON AND CANAL ST

The cobblestone streets of SoHo have become a haven for street photographers over the years due to the stylish folk who walk them. The sunsets in summer are epic.

SHOP

3SIXTEEN NY
190 ELIZABETH ST

3sixteen NY's signature jeans are crafted using custom fabrics from the legendary Kuroki Mills in Okayama, Japan. Their Nolita location is a space you'll appreciate not only for its goods, but its character too.

AIMÉ LEON DORE
214 MULBERRY ST

The NYC post-streetwear brand's Mulberry flagship is an ever-evolving space that has garnered a dedicated community. There's also a cafe inside that serves up delicious Greek cookies and pastries.

MCNALLY JACKSON BOOKS
134 PRINCE ST

Their cult following has led to recent expansions in several locations around the city. The newest hub, just down the road from their original, still holds the magic.

NOLITA MARKET
PRINCE ST

There are lots of unique finds at this artisans' market. It also makes for a leisurely stroll along bustling Prince Street Friday through Sunday.

EAT

LA ESQUINA
114 KENMARE ST

This iconic eatery and bar on the corner of Kenmare and Lafayette streets has a cafe and casual taquería up top and a secret brasserie down below. The grilled-octopus tostadas are top notch.

JACK'S WIFE FREDA
226 LAFAYETTE ST

Having originally opened on Lafayette Street in 2011, they recently moved just up the corner (among several other locations around the city), but this spot takes the cake with Parisian-cafe-inspired outdoor seating.

FANELLI CAFE
94 PRINCE ST

The historic restaurant and bar is considered the city's second-oldest food-and-drink establishment in the same locale. It has operated under various owners since 1847, but its lively spirit lives on.

LITTLE PRINCE
199 PRINCE ST

This intimate French bistro, decorated with globe pendant lamps and a handpainted ceramic tile floor, is pure chic. Grab a seat at the ten-person bar for a cosy experience.

PLAY

BOTANICA
47 E HOUSTON ST

A former home to iconic music venue The Knitting Factory, Botanica still attracts SoHo's elite music and art crowd with its loud music and dim mood lighting.

THE GARRET COCTELERÍA
349 BROOME ST

This tropical-inspired bar serves Caribbean-style bites and is pure camp! Visit during the cold months, as it will warm you right up!

CLUB ROOM
AT THE SOHO GRAND HOTEL
310 W BROADWAY

The swanky two-room bar is a perfect mix of old and new, melding Downtown style and old-New-York gentility. Filled with sultry live jazz in the early evening, the sound turns to dance-inducing disco later in the night.

JIMMY
15 THOMPSON ST

Set 18 storeys high in SoHo, Jimmy is a rooftop bar that features some impressive views of Downtown and features one of the few outdoor pool decks in town.

GUEROS
605 PROSPECT PL, CROWN HEIGHTS

"I grew up in Crown Heights and there is this place called Gueros there that me and my friends always go to. They have the best fish tacos and it's just a very community-oriented, down-to-earth place."

SAMUEL IN SOHO

SOHO

LEFT BANK BOOKS
41 PERRY ST, GREENWICH VILLAGE

"Left Bank Books has cosy vibes and some really great finds. It's an eclectic collection of used and rare books from literature, art, fashion – that kind of stuff."

NOLITA AND SOHO

<u>PLAY</u>

LINCOLN CENTER FOR THE PERFORMING ARTS
LINCOLN CENTER PLAZA, UPPER WEST SIDE

"I love all you can do at Lincoln Center: watch the ballet, listen to music, or just hang out."

BRENDA IN TRIBECA

The bustling streets of New York are like a symphony in full swing. But if you're looking for somewhere cosier, these places hit the right note.

VIBE

Rhapsody in blue

MEZZROW
163 W 10TH ST
Compared to its older brother, Smalls Jazz Club, Mezzrow is more of a jazz piano room. It's a relaxed environment: chilled and upscale, but not snooty.

CANARY CLUB
303 BROOME ST
Serving New Orleans-inspired bites and drinks, their basement music lounge comes alive with a variety of acts, including the likes of Jon Batiste.

MARKET HOTEL
1140 MYRTLE AVE
This concert hall above Mr Kiwi's overlooks an elevated subway platform on the 2nd floor, giving you a truly epic New York backdrop during shows.

DOWNTOWN MUSIC GALLERY
13 MONROE STREET
A long-running record store with an international reputation, it's also equipped as a performance space for avant-garde, jazz and contemporary musicians.

MARIE'S CRISIS CAFE
59 GROVE ST
This showtunes-only piano bar is a great night out. Here, all are welcome to take a seat and sing their little heart out.

WILLIAMSBURG MUSIC CENTER
367 BEDFORD AVENUE
One of Brooklyn's last remaining Black-owned jazz clubs, WMC feels like you're in someone's living room witnessing magic.

WASHINGTON SQUARE PARK DOG RUN
52 WASHINGTON SQUARE S, GREENWICH VILLAGE

"I'm a dog walker from the Bronx, so I do a lot of walking, especially here in the West Village. I love it around here, everyone is just so happy and cheerful and there are dogs everywhere. These guys love the dog run!"

LESLIE IN THE WEST VILLAGE

WEST VILLAGE

JOE'S COFFEE
141 WAVERLY PL, WEST VILLAGE

*"When I'm in the city, I love Joe's Coffee.
The people who work here are cute!"*

RICHARD IN THE WEST VILLAGE

WEST VILLAGE

CHRISTOPHER ST
BETWEEN WEST ST AND 6TH AVE

*"I just came out today, so yay!
Thought it would be appropriate to
come down to Christopher Street."*

ANNA-LISA IN THE WEST VILLAGE

West Village

Despite being small, the West Village is the kind of neighbourhood you can easily spend a day wandering around. Its bohemian occupants may be long gone, but their spirit lives on through the LGBTQ+ community, who have given the streets new life.

LOOK

IFC CENTER
323 6TH AVE

This art-house movie theatre is one of the few places in the city where you can see screenings of independent films from around the world. Their regular Q+A events with cast and directors are also not to be missed.

CHRISTOPHER PARK
38-64 CHRISTOPHER ST

Located across from iconic gay bar The Stonewall Inn, Christopher Park has been at the centre of the LGBTQ+ rights movement since the historic 1969 Stonewall riots, where a police raid on the bar prompted an uprising.

HUDSON RIVER
GREENWAY
WEST ST

The greenway runs from Pier 45 up to Little Island, one of the city's newest parks. You can walk the length, or grab a bike. Either way, there are some great views.

NEW OHIO THEATRE
154 CHRISTOPHER ST

This off-off-Broadway theatre specialises in bold new works from the diverse independent theatre community in New York.

SHOP

CASA MAGAZINES
22 8TH AVE

Truly a mecca for magazine lovers, this tiny space is filled with titles from around the world. If you can't find your favourite though, owner Mohammed Ahmed will go above and beyond to get it.

THREE LIVES
& COMPANY
154 W 10TH ST

A "reader's bookshop" if there ever was one, this snug neighbourhood haven was cited as "a pocket of civility" by the Greenwich Village Historical Society.

GOODS FOR THE STUDY
50 W 8TH ST

From the owner of McNally Jackson Books comes a stationery store with all the tools to get your workspace in shape. Print enthusiasts will love their extensive selection of pens and paper goods.

OLFACTORY NYC
355 BLEECKER ST

Bleecker Street is not the thriving shopping district it once was, but the experimental shops popping up in the area are worth a visit. At Olfactory you can craft a one-of-a-kind fragrance in their Scent Studio.

EAT

BONSIGNOUR
35 JANE ST

This quaint cafe off
8th Avenue has earned
its local community's
patronage by dishing up
over 30 years' worth
of home-cooked meals.
Order an iced tea and
croissant, and grab a
stool outside.

THE WAVERLY INN
AND GARDEN
16 BANK ST

The Inn draws in a handful
of faithfuls who maintain
a certain constancy.
Opened as Ye Waverly Inn
& Garden in 1920, this
tucked-away spot has
always served chicken
potpie, and attracted a
literary-bohemian crowd.

JOE'S PIZZA
7 CARMINE ST

An institution since 1975,
Joe's Pizza is the place
to grab a quality slice.
You'll most likely be
greeted by a queue, but
don't let that scare you
off - they're quick.

VIA CAROTA
51 GROVE ST

This Italian trattoria
is as New York as you'll
find. It can be hard to
get a seat, but if you
do, the Cacio e Pepe
is heavenly.

PLAY

CUBBYHOLE
281 W 12TH ST

You won't fall short of
queer bars in the village
- the iconic Stonewall
Inn, Ty's, Rockbar -
but a few blocks north
sits a lesbian bar where
everybody knows your name,
or at least they will
after a few cheap drinks
and good jukebox picks.

THE MONSTER
80 GROVE ST

There is something for
everyone at this classic
queer hangout, from a piano
bar upstairs that's always
filled with local talent
to the basement level with
drag shows and dancing.

SMALLS JAZZ CLUB
183 W 10TH ST

Small seems to be a theme
in the West Village, and
this jazz club leans right
into it. Smalls Jazz
Club is the real deal,
showcasing big talent in
a tiny, low-key space.

DANTE WEST VILLAGE
551 HUDSON ST

This place is the go-to
for an aperitivo. The
establishment's obsession
with the negroni inspired
the creation of a menu
entirely dedicated to the
drink - the Chocolate
Negroni is a must!

PLAY

FORT TILDEN BEACH
CENTER RD, ROXBURY

"It's a really nice place. There's no signal so you just shut off. It's very peaceful."

HAI IN THE WEST VILLAGE

WASHINGTON SQUARE PARK

PLAY

PIECES BAR
8 CHRISTOPHER ST, WEST VILLAGE

"It's only my third time in the city but I love Pieces Bar! What can I say? I love me some drag!"

TAYCE NEAR MADISON SQUARE PARK

WEST VILLAGE

ABINGDON SQUARE PARK
HUDSON ST, WEST VILLAGE

"I'm always grabbing some reading material at Casa Magazines and heading across the street to Abingdon Square Park: it's so peaceful."

SENAMI IN THE WEST VILLAGE

It's easy to feel inspired in New York. You could visit the city's most famous museums and galleries, but these smaller places pack a punch.

I wanna feel something

ICP MUSEUM
79 ESSEX ST
Spread over two storeys, you'll find photography that demonstrates the power of the image from photographers worldwide.

LESLIE-LOHMAN MUSEUM OF ART
26 WOOSTER ST
This foundation collects, preserves and exhibits art in various forms created by and/or about LGBTQ+ themes, issues and people.

THE DRAWING CENTER
35 WOOSTER ST
Drawing, in both historical and contemporary forms, is the focus here. Their public programs will have you reaching for a pencil.

THE PUBLIC THEATER
425 LAFAYETTE ST
Formerly The Astor Library, this impressive building houses five theatres plus Joe's Pub, a cabaret-style venue with shows from live music to soloists and spoken word.

HAPPY MEDIUM
49 MARKET ST
An art cafe where you can order drinks and snacks, as well as art supplies, tableside. The best part? You don't need to clean up.

HENRY STREET
TWO BRIDGES
In 2020, a cluster of galleries on Henry Street all signed multi-year leases; it has since become the city's new experimental art hub.

WHITNEY MUSEUM OF AMERICAN ART
99 GANSEVOORT ST, WEST VILLAGE

"Museums, any in the city, make my heart beat. I love art. The Whitney always has something amazing on."

MARY IN SOHO

EAST VILLAGE

B&H DAIRY

127 2ND AVE, EAST VILLAGE

"B&H Dairy in the East Village is an old-school, circa 1940s, kosher diner that's always worth a visit."

SARAH IN THE WEST VILLAGE

EAST VILLAGE

TOMPKINS SQUARE PARK
E 10TH ST, EAST VILLAGE

"Tompkins Square Park, bro. I grew up around here."

East Village

Once the epicentre of the city's punk scene, St. Marks Place in the East Village has, for the most part, stayed true to its roots. Still offbeat and raw on this main strip and the surrounding streets, you're in for a good time – come day or night.

ASTOR PL
SUBWAY STATION

3RD AVE

COOPER SQ

2ND AVE

1ST AVE

AVENUE A

E 12TH ST

E 11TH ST

E 10TH ST

E 9TH ST

ST. MARKS PLACE

E 7TH ST

E 6TH ST

E 5TH ST

E 4TH ST

E HOUSTON ST

TOMPKINS
SQUARE
PARK

LOWER
EAST SIDE
▼

LOOK

ARTS ON SITE
12 ST. MARKS PL
A female-led arts organisation hosting intimate performances by artists working in dance, music, visual art and theatre. "The Performance Party Event" is a fun, immersive experience that brings art to life!

PS122
GALLERY
150 1ST AVE
This not-for-profit space in the East Village champions emerging and under-represented artists, and holds many thought-provoking exhibitions.

NEW YORK THEATRE
WORKSHOP
79 E 4TH ST
Their first production was a two-year developmental workshop of Jonathan Larson's *Rent* back in 1994. It's worth booking a ticket to one of their current productions for that history alone.

VILLAGE EAST
BY ANGELIKA
181-189 2ND AVE
Part of the former Yiddish Theatre District, this cinema was designed in the Moorish Revival style and screens art-house and commercial films.

SHOP

A-1 RECORD SHOP
439 E 6TH ST
It's not difficult to find a good record shop in New York, but it's the soulful community that A-1 has attracted that makes this one so special.

PRINTED MATTER/
ST. MARKS
38 ST. MARKS PL
Located in the Swiss Institute, a not-for-profit arts organisation, Printed Matter's second location is a treasure trove of independently published books, zines and other artistic matter. The exhibitions at SI are always worth a look, too.

SEARCH AND DESTROY
25 ST. MARKS PL
A densely packed vintage shop that's punk-rock to its core — studded belts, bondage gear and gas masks aplenty — but which also has a large range of vintage band tees from decades and genres past.

EAST VILLAGE BOOKS
99 ST. MARKS PL
Be ready to be greeted by creaky floorboards and the scent of old paper. That rare book you've been looking for all your life may just be waiting here.

EAT

TAQUERIA
ST. MARKS PLACE
79 ST. MARKS PL

This dive-y bar/eatery has
margaritas and Mexican
food so cheap, you'll
think you're in St. Marks
Place circa 1990. Plus,
who doesn't love unlimited
chips and salsa?

PORTO RICO
IMPORTING CO.
40 1/2 ST. MARKS PL

If you love the smell of
coffee, there is over
thirty years' worth of
coffee aroma lingering in
the air at Porto Rico!
You can buy sacks of the
stuff at this location
or at two of their other
stores in the city.

CAFE MOGADOR
101 ST. MARKS PL

This St. Marks classic
draws a bohemian crowd
with its Moroccan-inspired
cuisine and great indoor
and outdoor vibes. It's
a popular brunch spot, but
also the perfect place on
a balmy summer night.

CHELI
19 ST. MARKS PL

Specialising in
Shanghai cuisine, this
fantastically elaborate
dining room with bamboo-
hut-like booths serves an
amazing giant steamed bun.

PLAY

THE COCK
93 2ND AVE

Not for the faint hearted,
this unapologetic gay dive
bar hosts theme parties,
go-go dancers and DJs in
the main room, with the
basement serving as a dark
room — if you know, you
know. Look for the neon
sign of a rooster.

CLUB CUMMING
505 EAST 6TH ST

Don't let its unmarked
facade fool you, as
its lavish interiors
frequently host various
cabaret shows, dance
parties and drag
performances. You may even
catch its namesake on
stage from time to time.

INTERNATIONAL BAR
102 1ST AVE.

A small, old-school dive
bar that draws locals
who like unpretentious
drinks. Some might even
say it's a cushy spot on a
cold winter's night — the
lighting is on point!

NO BAR AT
THE STANDARD
25 COOPER SQ

The idea behind the name
is No Holds Barred, and
they deliver. This hotel
bar welcomes everyone, but
their queer line-up is what
makes for a chaotic night!

CHOLO & SONS BAKERY
3825 WHITE PLAINS RD, THE BRONX

"I love Antigua bread shops. They have a Sunday bread, but extra rich, made with vegetable shortening or lard. It's a Caribbean thing. Amazing!"

MALCHIJAH IN THE WEST VILLAGE

EAST VILLAGE

THE SULTAN ROOM
234 STARR ST, BUSHWICK

"My favourite area is Tompkins Square Park. But the best venue to catch a show has to be The Sultan Room in Brooklyn – the atmosphere, the lighting, all that stuff is killer."

REX IN SOHO

NOHO

MARYLOU
41 ST. MARKS PL, EAST VILLAGE

"Marylou in the East Village has great French food and a really relaxed vibe where you can eat, drink and hang out with your friends."

JEREMIAH IN THE LOWER EAST SIDE

With a population of over eight million, you'll never be lonely in New York, but sometimes it's nice to escape the crowds and spend time solo.

The only living boy in New York

COLEMAN SKATEPARK
62 MONROE ST
A visit to this skate park under the Manhattan Bridge can be meditative, with the repetitive sound of wheels hitting the pavement above and below you.

JANE STREET GARDEN
36 JANE ST
A tiny park on busy 8th Avenue where you'll be engulfed by trees and forget where you are.

THE HIGH LINE
W 14TH ST
Although filled with tourists on the best of days, the key to peace on the High Line is to visit on a rainy day.

PIER 45
353 WEST ST
It's far enough out to feel you've left the bustling city behind you. Come here for the great views of Lower Manhattan.

MEOW PARLOUR
46 HESTER ST
If you'd rather spend time with cats than humans, this place offers by-the-hour play time, plus refreshments.

THE FERRY
VARIOUS LOCATIONS
It's cheap, hardly crowded in the evenings and you get to enjoy the sound of thrashing winds if you sit on the top deck.

WASHINGTON SQUARE PARK
WASHINGTON SQUARE, GREENWICH VILLAGE

"There's an old New York City vibe going on at Washington Square Park at the moment."

DAMION IN THE WEST VILLAGE

WILLIAMSBURG

BROWER PARK

BROOKLYN AVE AND PROSPECT PL, CROWN HEIGHTS

"Brower Park in Crown Heights. I love seeing the diversity of communities that use the park. Everything from people dancing, studying religions, even book clubs. You can witness everyday happenings and I love it."

JASMINE IN CHELSEA

WILLIAMSBURG

LUCKY DOG
303 BEDFORD AVE, WILLIAMSBURG

"I met my partner at a dog park. We go to Lucky Dog a lot because it's dog friendly."

JAMES IN WILLIAMSBURG

Williamsburg

Known as one of the birthplaces of the modern hipster, Williamsburg has been the poster child for gentrification over the last couple of decades. But it seems like the dust has almost settled and this melting pot of communities is finally coming into its own.

LOOK

DOMINO PARK
15 RIVER ST
Part of the larger
renovation and restoration
of the Domino Sugar
Refinery land, you can't
beat the views from this
waterfront park.

BATHHOUSE
103 N 10TH ST
In the basement level
of this 1930s factory,
you'll find a black-lit
hallway tunnelling through
a glass-enclosed chamber
with glowing tropical
plants, which leads you
to a modern-day spa that
ditches the white, minimal
aesthetic for something
dark, moody and sexy.

McCARREN PARK POOL
776 LORIMER ST
If you're visiting during
the summer months and
looking to cool down, this
Olympic-sized public pool
was revitalised in the
mid-2000s after becoming
derelict in the 80s. It's
a NYC landmark brought
back to its 1930s glory.

MIRIAM GALLERY
319 BEDFORD AVE
This gallery and
bookshop prides itself on
collaborating with the
artists and curators they
host, through exhibitions,
events and artist books.

SHOP

AMARCORD VINTAGE
FASHION
223 BEDFORD AVE
Expertly curated, high-end
vintage clothing presented
as if it was in a Midtown
department store. Even
their window display would
put Bergdorf Goodman
to shame.

THE MINI MALL
218 BEDFORD AVE
Williamsburg's only
shopping mall might be
mini, but it offers
a variety of vintage
boutiques selling
antiques, books and
jewellery - all with that
Brooklyn twist.

SPOONBILL
BOOKS
218 BEDFORD AVE
In The Mini Mall you'll
find this quaint bookstore
offering new and used
books. There's a focus on
art and design, theory,
literature and poetry.

TEN ICHI MART
& DELI
188 BERRY ST
Get a little taste of
Japan in Brooklyn with
freshly made Japanese
snacks, bubble tea and an
impressive selection of
packaged goods you really
don't see that much of
outside of Japan.

EAT

ALLSWELL
124 BEDFORD AVE
This laid-back
Williamsburg tavern has
classic American pub
written all over it.
There's a daily menu
served on a communal
table, but you can't
beat their one fixture:
a classic cheeseburger!

7 GRAIN ARMY
88 ROEBLING ST
Some might think that
delicious and gluten free
don't go together, but
this low-key neighbourhood
bakery is concocting magic
with their gooey, jam-
filled Blueberry Oat Muffin
– it's out of this world!

LA BICYCLETTE BAKERY
667 DRIGGS AVE
On the more traditional
side, this charming
bakery serves a menu of
French classics including
croissants, pain au
chocolat, quiche Lorraine,
and ham and cheese
baguettes. You're welcome.

SUNDAY IN BROOKLYN
348 WYTHE AVE
This brunch spot is known
for more than the food.
The natural light, exposed
beams, marble tabletops
and big bar make for an
appetising Instagram shot.
Just go with it.

PLAY

SPECTACLE
124 S 3RD ST
A collectively run
screening space in a
former bodega, featuring
overlooked films, offbeat
gems, contemporary art,
radical polemics and live
performances.

VITAL CLIMBING GYM
221 N 14TH ST
If walking the streets
of New York isn't enough
activity for you, this
impressive warehouse
conversion has some pretty
epic walls for you to
climb, even on the rooftop!

PETE'S CANDY STORE
709 LORIMER ST
This pocket-sized bar has a
little bit of everything,
but it's the free music
in the train-car shaped
performance space that's
a real treat. See various
acts perform every night.

CARIBBEAN SOCIAL
CLUB *AKA* TOÑITA'S
244 GRAND ST
One of the last remaining
Puerto Rican social clubs
in the city, it's a space
frozen in a time when the
neighbourhood was the
Puerto Rican enclave known
as "Los Sures". Saturday
nights are a dance party
like no other. Wear
comfortable shoes.

KING TAI
1095 BERGEN ST, CROWN HEIGHTS

"King Tai is a great bar that puts on some even greater events."

NOEL IN WILLIAMSBURG

WILLIAMSBURG

HUMAN RELATIONS
1067 FLUSHING AVE, EAST WILLIAMSBURG

*"Besides my girlfriend's shop [Studio Dem],
I love Human Relations. It's a used-book store,
the kind that doesn't exist much anymore.
The people there really know their stuff."*

JORDAN IN WILLIAMSBURG

WILLIAMSBURG

MONSIGNOR MCGOLRICK PARK
RUSSELL ST AND NASSAU AVE, GREENPOINT

"Love having ice cream at around 7:15pm on a summer night in Monsignor McGolrick Park in Greenpoint."

JAE AND JAY IN WILLIAMSBURG

Although Katz's Deli is a staple casual dining experience, there are other old and new eateries where you can get a cheap thrill, too.

I'll have what she's having...

EMPIRE DINER
210 10TH AVE
The original closed in 2010, but after numerous attempts at a revival, this iconic Art Deco diner has found its place with spins on American dishes, coffee and cocktails.

COURT STREET GROCER
540 LAGUARDIA PL
Grab a Jersey-style pork roll on a Big Marty's potato bun and enjoy it while you people-watch in Washington Square Park.

AUJLA'S INDIAN COFFEE HOUSE
56 HESTER ST
Inside Bode Tailor Shop, you'll find this authentic Indian teahouse serving cardamom-infused coffee and fish sandwiches.

LA BONBONNIERE
28 8TH AVE
This place is the quintessential New York diner — a cheap and cheerful menu, old-school atmosphere and a wild mix of people.

GOLDEN DINER
123 MADISON ST
A modern take on the diner by Momofuku Ko alum Samuel Yoo that caters to the tastes of the Chinese, Latin and veggie-happy neighborhood.

KIKI'S
130 DIVISION ST
Don't let the old printing shop sign with Chinese script throw you off — the food here is 100% traditional Greek. Order the saganaki, perfectly doused in honey and lemon.

KRISPY KREME
1601 BROADWAY, TIMES SQUARE

"There's a big Krispy Kreme in the city that's open 24/7, what else could you want?"

NETA IN WILLIAMSBURG

WILLIAMSBURG

BROOKLYN BRIDGE PARK
334 FURMAN ST, DUMBO

"Brooklyn Bridge Park has beautiful sunsets."

"I like to go on field trips there with my classmates and have picnics!"

ADA AND CLINT IN COBBLE HILL

WILLIAMSBURG

FRONT GENERAL STORE
143 FRONT ST, DUMBO

*"They have some really good vintage finds.
And a bunch of homewares and stuff.
It's got a retro vibe."*

KRIS IN DUMBO

Cobble Hill & Boerum Hill

These side-by-side neighbourhoods in the heart of Brooklyn are among the borough's most picturesque. But don't let their brownstone-lined streets fool you – there's still plenty of edge to be found here.

1. THE INVISIBLE DOG ART CENTER 2. ACE HOTEL BROOKLYN
3. COBBLE HILL CINEMAS 4. ROULETTE INTERMEDIUM
5. THE BROOKLYN CIRCUS 6. BOOKS ARE MAGIC 7. CABIN MODERN
8. MERCADO CENTRAL 9. PLANTED CAFE 10. CAFE VOLKAN
11. BROOKLYN FARMACY AND SODA FOUNTAIN 12. CUBANA CAFE
13. BARELY DISFIGURED 14. SOMEDAY BAR 15. BROOKLYN INN
16. MIA'S BROOKLYN BAKERY

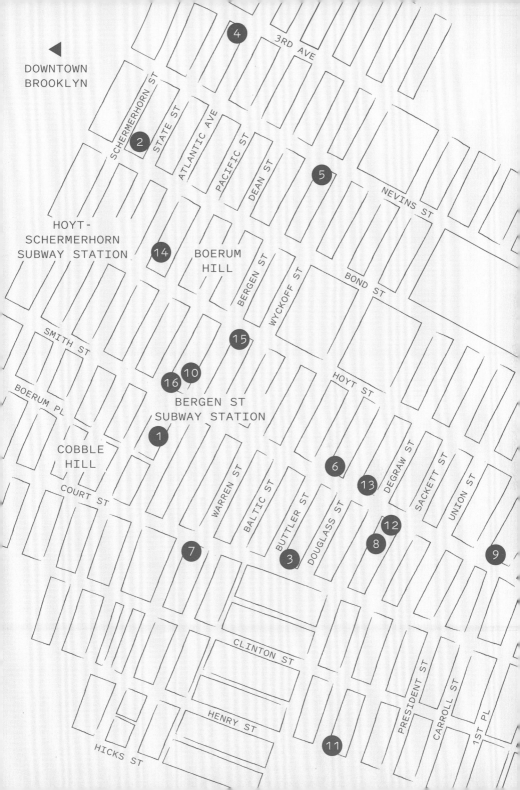

LOOK

THE INVISIBLE DOG
ART CENTER
51 BERGEN ST

This museum and arts centre
is a hidden treasure. It
plays host to performances,
exhibitions and artists
in residence. They also
have two Airbnbs filled
with said art that run to
support the arts centre.

ACE HOTEL
BROOKLYN
252 SCHERMERHORN ST

The famed hotel's
Brooklyn location is close
to everything Cobble Hill
and Boerum Hill have to
offer, but it's the fun
and engaging exhibitions
and events they host
inside the hotel that make
it worth visiting.

COBBLE HILL CINEMAS
265 COURT ST

The marquee is updated
by hand and the ticket
guy tears your ticket at
the door. This theatre is
analog in almost every way,
giving you a classic movie
theatre experience.

ROULETTE
509 ATLANTIC AVE

Housed in a Beaux-Arts
concert hall on the edge
of Boerum Hill, catch one
of over 120 experimental
music, dance and
intermedia performances.

SHOP

THE BROOKLYN
CIRCUS
150 NEVINS ST

Known for its varsity
jackets and appreciation
for vintage garments,
creative director Ouigi
Theodore brings a modern
take to classic American
menswear. His HQ is an
incredible ode to what the
brand is all about.

BOOKS ARE MAGIC
225 SMITH ST

Owned and operated by
American author Emma
Straub and her husband
Michael Fusco-Straub,
this new generation
of bookstores is well
curated, offers trendy
merch and hosts great
events almost every night.

CABIN MODERN
220 COURT ST

Owned by another husband-
and-wife team, Cabin
Modern sell restored
mid-century modern
furnishings, as well as
original hand-printed
textiles and prints.

MERCADO CENTRAL
354 DEGRAW ST

One of countless "mom-
and-pop shops" in the
neighbourhood, drop in for
authentic Spanish imports
and New York's largest
selection of tinned fish.

EAT

PLANTED
333 SMITH ST
As well as locally made,
organic, vegan (with some
protein options) and
gluten-free fare, this
cafe sells houseplants and
edibles. The brownie bites
are phenomenal.

CAFE VOLKAN
85 BERGEN ST
Everything a neighbourhood
coffee shop needs — a good
basic menu, genuinely kind
service, popularity with
the locals and, of course,
a great cup of coffee!

BROOKLYN FARMACY
AND SODA FOUNTAIN
513 HENRY ST
This old-school soda
shop is as charming as it
gets. They serve sundaes,
egg creams and all sorts
of other comfort foods
in a former apothecary
store with its original
tin-pressed ceilings and
mosaic-tiled floors.

CUBANA CAFE
272 SMITH ST
Sometimes, it's not
only about the food,
but about the energy
of a space. This Cuban
restaurant has both -
and even solo visitors
will feel like they're
being welcomed to dine
with friends.

PLAY

BARELY DISFIGURED
257 SMITH ST
Despite the sign on the
front window, this is not
a brothel (but it does
hint at the location's
past). Instead, it's
a new favourite amongst
locals, as well as
cocktail aficionados.

SOMEDAY BAR
364 ATLANTIC AVE
For a "quieter" end of
town, this bar proves that
this city really never
sleeps. 1am on a Monday
night still sees people
rolling in. A chill space
with great bartenders.

BROOKLYN INN
148 HOYT ST
Old-school watering hole
with a beautiful 19th-
century wood bar, low-key
atmosphere, a jukebox
and a pool table. It's an
ideal neighbourhood bar,
if there ever was one.

MIA'S BROOKLYN
BAKERY
139 SMITH ST
If you're looking for a
late-night hangout, minus
the booze, this dessert
bar has you covered.
The menu seems endless,
offering delicious
sweets along with a few
savouries. But make sure
you know your limit.

JULIANA'S PIZZA
19 OLD FULTON ST, DUMBO

"Juliana's Pizza has nice family vibes, great wine and, obviously, great pizza."

OMAR IN BROOKLYN HEIGHTS

COBBLE HILL AND NOHO

PROSPECT PARK ZOO
450 FLATBUSH AVE, PROSPECT PARK

*"We've always lived in Park Slope.
It's a great neighbourhood. We love
the zoo in Prospect Park."*

KARA IN WILLIAMSBURG

LOWER EAST SIDE

SHOP

SOHO
SOUTH OF HOUSTON ST

*"To be honest, I just like shopping around here.
I just picked up a new pair of shoes!"*

JAKE IN SOHO

The city is full of wonderful places to find the printed word. Here are some iconic plus new independent bookshops worth browsing.

Let's get lit

STRAND BOOK STORE
828 BROADWAY

A truly iconic bookstore that is always worth a visit. With 18 miles of 2.5 million new and used books, spread over four floors, you can spend an entire afternoon here.

BUNGEE SPACE
13 STANTON ST

This bookstore not only has great art books, but the building also houses a coffee shop, clothing store, exhibition space, and a publishing and podcast studio.

HOUSING WORKS
BOOKSTORE
126 CROSBY ST

Book sales provide crucial funding for people living with and affected by HIV/AIDS. All their stock is donated and the store is almost entirely staffed by volunteers.

BOOK THUG NATION
100 N 3RD ST

This tiny store with an impressive selection of fiction, film and philosophy books came to be when three sidewalk booksellers decided to ditch the streets.

DASHWOOD BOOKS
33 BOND ST A

If you'd rather look at pretty pictures, this wonderful place is devoted exclusively to photography books, including rare and out-of-print titles.

KARMA BOOKSTORE
136 E 3RD ST

Sitting in the beloved former St. Marks Bookshop, Karma stays true to the Downtown arts scene, stocking artists' books, along with used and rare titles that focus on contemporary art, photography and painting.

BOOK CLUB
197 E 3RD ST, EAST VILLAGE

"There's a coffee shop/bookstore called Book Club that has some outdoor seating, and it's just chill. Great place to get inspired."

EMANUEL IN THE EAST VILLAGE

WILLIAMSBURG AND NOLITA

LOOK

CARVER HOUSES
1475 MADISON AVE, SPANISH HARLEM

"My family is from Spanish Harlem. I spend a lot of time there, especially at the Carver project."

JEM IN UNION SQUARE

CHELSEA AND COBBLE HILL

"I'm from Puerto Rico.
It's my first day in New York City.
I'm here to be a model."

NOMA IN DUMBO

Acknowledgements

Thank you to the people of New York, old friends and new, who have made this wonderful city feel like my second home. I may never earn that "New Yorker" badge, but it's an honour to get to photograph you.

Thank you to Paul and Smith Street Books for publishing my work in the printed form – I am forever grateful to you.

And to Josh, thank you for being my home.

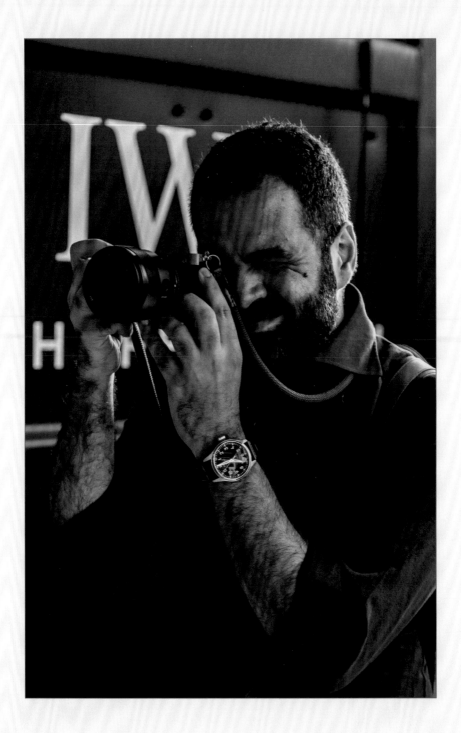

The Author

Giuseppe Santamaria is a photographer and designer originally from Toronto, Canada. He resides in Sydney, Australia, with his partner, Josh, and their dog, Sebastian.

He is the author of :
Men In This Town (2014),
Women In This Town (2015),
Alone In A Crowd (2017) and
A Decade of Men's Street Style (2021).

Follow his work at
giuseppesantamaria.studio and
gsinthistown.com, and his life in photos
on Instagram @giuseppeinthistown

PUBLISHED IN 2023 BY SMITH STREET BOOKS
NAARM (MELBOURNE) | AUSTRALIA
SMITHSTREETBOOKS.COM

ISBN: 978-1-92275-453-0

SMITH STREET BOOKS RESPECTFULLY ACKNOWLEDGES THE WURUNDJERI
PEOPLE OF THE KULIN NATION, WHO ARE THE TRADITIONAL OWNERS OF THE
LAND ON WHICH WE WORK, AND WE PAY OUR RESPECTS TO THEIR ELDERS
PAST AND PRESENT.

PUBLISHER: PAUL MCNALLY
ART DIRECTION: GIUSEPPE SANTAMARIA
EDITOR: TAHLIA ANDERSON
PROOFREADER: ROWENA ROBERTSON

PRINTED & BOUND IN CHINA BY C&C OFFSET PRINTING CO., LTD.

BOOK 280
10 9 8 7 6 5 4 3 2 1